AMERICAN ANGST

C.A. Fraser

American Angst

Copyright © 2019 by C.A. Fraser

ISBN: 978-0-578-45502-0

Book cover by: cafraserpub@gmail.com

Dedication:

To the middle.

You know who you are.

We need you.

Use your voice.

AMERICAN

ANGST

Yes,
I
Am
Talking
To
You.

Split...

You.
Me.
Both
Hold our own
Way of thinking.

Refusing to
See the light in the other's voice
Only perceiving the unknown threat to
Our way of life.
Forgetting the lesson of our
Early years.

Judge not.
Instead stubborn
We cling unmoving
To our doom.

Let

Me

Break

The

News.

BORDER WALLS

Steel and concrete structures
Erected by small minds
To hide from imagined threats
And keep the "others" out.
Useless endeavors.
Sowing destruction.
Failing protection.

Only ever creating division.

Why can't we talk anymore?

Trans Conversational

It is
How I Feel.
It is
Who I am…?

Help me understand
Why
Dysphoria… Dysmorphia
Overcomes Biology.

It is
Not that easy.
I know.
There is a difference in my mind.

How at four or fifteen
Do you know?
Your life has just begun.
Please wait…

No…

We

1

Are

Learn Damnit!

Welcome!
Come in! Come in!
It will be fun!
Cookies
Fun time!
Recess…

Get back inside!
Sit down!
Be quiet!
Time to learn.
I said
Be Quiet.
Focus.
No daydreams
Here.
I will not
Ask again.
That's it!
Go
To the
Principal!

How   Much

Is

Enough?

The Price…

Take your medicine,

But pay the bill.

A forced choice between life and death.

How much to sacrifice

Before accepting the inevitable has come

Too soon.

Loved ones fight to

Provide the

Funds.

Refusing to lose.

Bake sales morphed to social media pleas.

As the weakness grows and the battle draws

You step onto the path.

Paying the price.

Who

Is

At

Fault?

Walt...

What?

Premature Death…

They died.

At the hands of illness shot from a barrel

The lead tearing life away.

We have sought to control the means.

Knowing that must be the answer.

Blind to the

Mind behind the gun.

Ignoring the human pulling

Death into our lives prematurely.

Instead renewing an argument from

Two centuries ago.

Time insists we remove the stigma

Or watch the helpless

Die.

When did

Food replace

My life?

Obese...

We are fat.

No, I am not sorry.

It is an epidemic.

It does not make you

Less.

It makes life harder.

But....

No big is not.

Beautiful.

Do not cry foul.

This is not persecution.

It is concern for you.

And me.

I do not want to lose

You.

Please help me.

Please help you.

Do You Understand What You Gave?

Eight Hours....

Eight hours plus.
Given in exchange
For the chance to exist.

Is this existence?
Doing an unseen
Cabal's bidding.

Grinding.

Relinquishing your
Chance at happiness with
Every moment that passes.

Unappreciated. Used until
There is nothing left.
Then discarded. Wait...
That's right laid off.
Severed from that which
You gave all.

Now free.
Do not fall into the same,
Again.
Search for purpose.

Find your life.

It is harmless...

Right?

Visual Stimuli…

But it turns me on.
The carnal acts.
Get me off. Satisfy the urge…
It is a mere touch away.
In a moment I can be
Immersed in a Fantasy…
Giving consent to the acts unfolding.
Embracing the darkness
Present in this so-called smut.
Abetting foul players.
Who abuse the unwilling.
Profiting off rampant libidos.

The guilt floods as the climax fades.

Weapons

Of

Mass

Destruction

WMD...

News:

Paper. TV. Radio.
Website. Social Media.
All cloaked.
Pretending to inform.
Denying
Their true intent.
To distract,
Mislead,

CONTROL.

A cycle of
Twenty-four hours.
Quick moving.
Preventing comprehension.
Concealing the true evil
Occurring daily.

Follow the money.

Rise Again?

Rebel…

The names for a flag.
That represents so much for so many.
Confederate. Dixie. Rebel.
Stars and bars.
(That one is wrong by the way)
What does it mean?
Heritage. War. History. Pride in.
Country?
What does it mean?
Lynching. Torture. Murder. Racism.
What does it mean?
Treason.

Do my words have any power?

Did you mean that...

Did you mean what you just said?

The hurt buried in your words.

I know how the roles are supposed to go

The lines clearly drawn to separate...

You and me.

I know what you have been told.

As have I....

But I don't

Believe that we are just the color of our skin.

Or the sum of our history.

You and I are equal.

Now all you must ask yourself is:

Did I mean what I just said?

BOOM!

Baby?

Generation Boom

You took what the greatest gave and

Squandered it day by day.

Conceding more and more

To the overpowered, the uber rich

In your selfish haste to have….

Forgetting the sacrifice made

As your desires Trump all.

Now blaming the future out of misplaced guilt.

You forget to look in the mirror….

Does your belief matter?

Does mine?

Oh God…

Real? Fake.

Powerful. Imagined?

The Almighty is being

Used.

To corrupt. To pervert.

To murder. To divide.

Replacing that

Which was given unknowingly

Away.

The god… … the goddess.

In each of us.

Stay

out

of

my

Bedroom?

Queer...

So, I like the same sex

Or maybe both.

How does that diminish me?

In your eyes

Why does that make me evil or damned?

Love disappears because of

Who shares my bed?

A book written by men ages ago

Restricts the ability to love?

Entitles you to use words and fists

To drive me away.

Degrade me and shout me down.

I refuse.

Really?

Me too…

You?

What about.

You?

Oh yeah….

Wait?

What about.

Me?

I have.

Life, love….

Challenges, desires….

Why am I

Not

Special?

Where is the chorus.

For me.

Me too...

We must

Survive.

Two Sides…

War!
We must fight the threat!
Our way will cease.
Line up!
Sacrifice metal, machines, bodies
To preserve the nebulous
Us.

Where are we?
On their land, taking the fight.
Securing resources, Forcing peace.
Surprised at insurrections
Our soldiers die.
The needed sacrifice to secure our,
Place in the world.

The threat is real.
Nefarious specters seek our
Fall. Wanting what we have built.
Attacking... never directly
Seeking allies to ensure we fail.
Creating conflict and human crises
Stretching us thin…
We must draw a line in the sand.

Or extend a hand...

They are watching.

What do you see?

Lines…

Ignoring all warnings,
We rush headlong into the bright future
Allowing the ease, the convenience, the tech
To break down our defense
To permeate our lives
Digging deeper until
Every picture, download, view, like, message,
Our conversation
Is monitored
Scoured by unseen eyes
With unknown intent
Violating our most intimate
Recording our most powerful
Enslaving our every moment.
The danger hidden in plain sight.

BIG

Business

Corporate Structure

Insanity in the guise of profit.
Drives the business of the day.
Process repeated
Again.
Regardless of results.

The truth hidden under layers of reports.
Money funneled to
Shareholders… or senseless purchases
In the guise of "growth".

The line of bureaucrats ever growing
Vainly struggling to garner favor.
Sacrificing people, integrity
Soul… for that elusive promotion.

Never realizing the foundation is crumbling,
The base weak...
Their fragile house set to

Fall.

**The
Politics
Of
Today.**

=

**The
Suffering
Of
Tomorrow?**

They never feel the pain…

Right, left.
Left, right.
Politicians, supposed representatives

Little more
Than sound bites propped up by
Talking heads.

Endless debates, sacrificing people
Without regret, never connecting decisions
Or lack of
To reality.

Cocooned in the guise of protector,
Savior of the people.

Clueless to the grief,
Never feeling the agony
They cause.

Your Choice.

Sanctity

You sit in judgement, as

The Almighty?

Preferring to demonize a choice,

Not understanding the agony of that moment.

The grief wrapped in her

Relief.

Instead you would have her carry to term.

Losing her life

Her dreams. Sacrificing everything.

Her sanity.

Or giving her child to an adoption…

Ring… Wrapped in the trappings of

Religion…. While drowning in

Money.

Understand she lives daily

Suffering with her choice.

Your vengeful heart and god are

Not needed here.

What

will

you

DO?

X Trapped

Smashed between two warring cultures

Interpreters of time and change.

Translating the Booming voice to the

Millennial mind.

Growing cynical. Disaffected.

Minds drifting to days of

Latchkey and grunge.

Somehow finding happiness as homes are lost,

Future retirement disappears and progeny remain.

Life circling as memories of a wall falling

Mingle with the reality of another rising.

The strings of destiny drawing tighter as

The gulf expands forcing a step

Forward into an

Uncertain future.

$$\frac{H_2O}{Pb}$$

Clean…

My thoughts flow

To a time when things were pure

Natural

Safe… Clean.

A time with laughter and joy.

Wealth

Health.

Then I take a sip and am jolted back to

Now.

To the failure as I stare at my cup

The Lead setting heavy in my gut.

What would make you forget everything?

Give up everything.

American Plague…

Foil litters the parks and lots.

Needles in the gutter.

Disposed of like the user,

Who briefly held it.

Junky. Loser. Son. Daughter.

Friend. Homeless. Lost.

Hopeless.

Utterly human….

Hero.

Sacrifice…

Purple Heart. Silver Star. Medal of Honor.

Brothers. Wounds. Family.

Pain. Money. Death…

All part of your sacrifice.

Returning Home to… Love and Hate.

Hugs. Spit. Protest. Celebration…

All part of your life now.

It marks you.

Seared into flesh and soul.

Few get it. Fewer Care.

It is a secret.

They can never know.

Where would you go?

What would you do?

If it happened to you?

Homeless?

Standing on the corner
A tattered cardboard sign
With a hastily scrawled message,
Matches equally tattered clothes.
Begging for
Money
Work
Food
Anything.

Driving by a passing
Observation.
How? Why?
What led to this?
Real or a scam?
Slowing down the glint of
Hope. Vanishes.
As I turn the corner.

**What
Boundaries?**

**What
Borders?**

The Web…

The flow of electrons

Translated into beauty, death and connection.

Allow links to endure.

The distance gone walls fall

Bringing community to the world

Threatening imaginary lines

Monitored by paper governments.

Revealing the hidden truth of

A connected humanity.

We are unstoppable.

Changing climate...

Changing future...

Home I don't remember…

Returning home.

Mountains tower in the distance

Always.

Now their permanence is joined by

Thick columns of smoke.

Images of trees explode, as fire tears through

The paper dry forest.

Rivers ankle deep,

Feed lakes once teeming with life

Now tepid and shrunk, the water flows to

Dwindling farms and dry towns

Adapting to the new

Normal.

Welcome Home.

Guess

What?

You thought...

You thought I wouldn't
Put you in here.

I wouldn't put your deeds
On display.

I wouldn't let the world see what and who you are.
You were wrong.

So here we are your acts laid bare.
The insidious plan exposed

For all to see.
You thought you were triumphant in your control.

That I was subdued.
A good little worker.

Providing and toiling daily for your cause.
You were so wrong.

I have seized the power
Found my voice

I will not be silenced
Any longer.

Buy

Buy

Buy

Buy

Buy

Buy

Buy

Buy

Buy

I will…

The hours tick by

Standing in line.

Waiting for the doors to open

All here to get the deal.

Overtired but excited at the prospect of

Saving…

Forgetting empathy as the manager begins

To let people in.

Going too slow.

The greed sparks something primal

Surging forward

People fall trampled in the rush

To get what everyone else wants

Just remember.

I will knock you down for that TV.

Stunning...

Beautiful...

Smart...

Strong...

Confident...

Unwanted Advances...

What do I say?

As you pass me on the street,
I cannot help but look…
You stop me at my work.

I catch your glance my way
What does it mean?
Did I catch your eye as well?

Or did my attention drive a spike of fear
In your heart.
My mind spins
I want to smile, to nod,
Anything to reassure you
That I see your beauty yes, but also

Your strength,

Your intelligence,

Your confidence.

And then you're gone.
Walking down the street as I stand
Struggling

What do I say?

Is

It

Too

Late...

Slow death...

A not so perfect union after all.
The liberty enshrined in the moment
Of our birth seized by those
In search of power.
The republic falling
To greed and corruption
Paralyzed by rhetoric.
The extremes ruling, the middle silent.
Watching the end.

Ancient

Ways

Ancient

Oil

Native Oil….

Black rivers flow unwanted

Under ancestral lands.

Threatening destruction moment by moment.

Profit won.

Overcoming lines of protest.

Now echoes carried on ancient winds

Joined by those long past

Their cries and chants invoking the magic of gods

And Earth in the vain

Hope to save their land.

Their way.

For the kids...

Oh, the Children…

How much evil has been done

In the name of children…

The instincts of parents turned

Used to commit atrocities

Limit speech, Censor Art

Burn books. But

What about the children?!

We must shelter them,

Protect them,

Hide them,

Stifle them.

In our haste to keep them

Safe.

Have we destroyed the only chance

They had….

So much for the...

American Dream.

The road to Paradise...

Let's do it again!
Hold on... Start Over...
Make it great... again!

Trust me I am here for the people!
I bring
Hope and Change!

I will revive this failing...
Well, if I am honest it is really
Not... failing....

But we must preserve it from...
Them!
Wait... not true either.

(Sigh)...

Honestly.
I say these things
To keep you at your station.

Distracted.
So you never realize

The road to Paradise is blocked.

Your

Holiday

Is

A

National

Security

Threat.

Safe Travels...

Up early
Do not be late.
Check your shit.
Where you from?
Yes, that line is for you.

Time to scan…
Shoes off, belts off
Step through, Arms up.
Better hope we don't find anything
We have rooms if need be….

Get to your gate!
See that guy with an escort.
Didn't listen.
Guess where he is going?

Ticket…Ticket…
Uh there are people waiting.
Wrong section step aside.
Now you can board.

Middle seat… of course
Pay attention
Belt, air, doors, slide.
Don't worry the flight will be smooth.

That? Just a little turbulence
Enjoy your flight!

Short Sentence...

Long...

Rapist…

Her clothes.

Her smile.

Somehow gave Permission.

Her innocence gone.

Life shattered.

She must move on.

But, not you.

No.

You are in prison.

How long?

That's all?

Well….

This is your cellmate.

…

He likes your smile...

How are you reading this?

Smart…
It rests in my hand
A repository of me
My knowledge and experience.
Tracking my every move.
Connecting me to the outside world
While recording everything.
Closer to me than any human.
It learns my habits.
Predicts my needs, my wants
My desires.
Demands my attention.
While freeing my mind.

What's
For
Dinner?

Edible…

When did it become dangerous

Just to eat…

We grow sick from

Salad.

Are poisoned by

Wine.

Every issue broadcast as a plague.

Striking fear, a cunning ruse

Designed to keep us hooked

On the processed

The prepackaged…

Failing to tell the simple truth of

Self-reliance...

There are some...

Hate…
Burning deeply.
Firmly wrapped in prejudice and
Fear.
Growing by day,
Twisting hearts with words and
Deeds.
Dividing, dividing and dividing
Yet again.
Until only strangers remain.
The world ends in terrified silence.

There are many...

Love...

It burns so brightly

At first.

Lighting up my mind

My heart.

Every minute draws us closer.

Creating a bond

Not possible before.

Not preparing

Me for when the flame

Dies.

Does it matter how I <u>lived</u>?

Expiring...

Forever came and failed to stay.
Now I stand terminal.
At the end most of life.
The play of experience and memory
Rending and soothing.
The grief a subtle ecstasy
I bath in as the moment passes
And light vanishes.
Leaving only vacant eyes.

Did I Fail?

Son…

I hope
I have
Been there
For you.

Provided the reason
The home, the love to
Sustain you.

Stood resolute in my support of
You.

Showing

Teaching

Demonstrating

What it is to be a good man.

Please

Never

Stop.

Scientific Method

Striving to understand our world
To explore the mysteries of our life
Expanding our knowledge
Our reach.
To the stars and the ocean depths
Now our gaze settles on world's beyond,
The secrets hidden within,
To the beginning of it all.
Seeking to understand…
Why we are here?

If there is a future...

Millennial Math…

We are shaped

By technology.

No longer shaping it

Symbiotic in our relationship.

A generation immersed in the future.

Almost a different species

With a sense of purpose

Utterly distinct

Cars, children, houses do not matter.

The Jones can't keep up anyway

Life

Experience

Friends and family matter.

We are here to change the world.

Running

On

Fumes.

Jam…

Glowing trails of red

Creep across the land.

Workers merging into the flow,

Economy made flesh

Each a cog, a fraction, a vital piece.

Flashes of orange signal change.

Progress measured in hours,

Stuck on an asphalt path.

Monitored continuously.

They drive

Minds numb, backs sore, feet aching.

Arriving home…Exhausted.

Until tomorrow

Just a reminder.

You forget…

You forget where the power lies.
In your quest for more
You forget the people who fought and died.
Who built this.
Their sweat and tears…
Their life and blood.
Given in exchange for
Better...
You forget these are the
Same people who will stand up.
Who will face you in that darkest moment.
Protect our family, our friends, our country
And take back what you stole.

Focus.

Distraction...

Race.
Gender.
Sex.
Religion.
Guns.
Abortion.
Jobs... The Economy.
Politics.
Borders.
These divide us.

A concentrated effort
To keep the people, separate….
To control them.
To focus wealth.
Consolidate power.
Preventing the truth from being realized.
The truth.
That Humanity is much more than any of these.

We the People.

LISTEN.

Reason.

Listen
To my voice.
Listen to me.
I know it is hard
The chaos, the constant
Static.
Wasted moments slowly draining you.
Taking the light that is your spirit...
Your soul...
And consuming it until
There is nothing left.
An empty husk withered with the decay of
The modern age.
You must fight!
Find the little things
To take back.
Own that which is yours.
Joy
Desire
Family
Purpose.
Refuse to give that last part.
The last inch that defines you.
Then take a foot.
A meter.
A mile.
Until you finally rule your world once more.
Now spread the word.

End.

LISTEN. Focus. Just a reminder. Running on fumes. If there is a future… Please never stop. Did I fail? Does it matter how I <u>lived</u>? There are many… There are some… What's for dinner? How are you reading this? Short Sentence… Long… Your Holiday Is A National Security Threat. So, much for the…American Dream. For the kids… Ancient Ways Ancient Oil Is it too late? Stunning… Beautiful… Smart… Strong… Confident… Unwanted Advances… Buy Buy Buy Buy Buy Buy Buy Buy Buy Guess What? Changing climate… Changing future… What Boundaries? What Borders? Where would you go? What would you do? If it happened to you? Hero. What would make you forget everything? Give up everything. H20/PB What will you DO? Your choice. The Politics of Today. = The Suffering of Tomorrow? Big Business They are watching. What do you see? We must survive. Really? Stay out of my bedroom? Does your belief matter? Does mine? BOOM! Baby? Do my words have any power? Rise Again? Weapons of Mass Destruction It is harmless… Right? Do You Understand What You Gave? When did food replace my life? Who is at fault? Wait… What? How much $ is enough? We are 1. Why can't we talk anymore? Let me break the news. Yes, I am talking to you. Dedication:

AMERICAN ANGST

www.ingramcontent.com/pod-product-compliance
Lightning Source LLC
Chambersburg PA
CBHW060123050426
42448CB00010B/2003